LIPSTICK & LOVE

Six soul memoirs from a modern day mystic

ISBN: 978-0-9812399-1-0

Published by Arias Press, Vancouver, Canada

www.ariaspress.com

Cover art by Morgen Matheson

First printing June 2009

Cataloguing data available from Library and Archives Canada

Dedicated to the Divine Feminine

with a special acknowledgement to Marie-Paule
who told me I would write this book.

And additional thanks to Mark for your unflagging
kindness and help.

Disclaimer

These stories are drawn from my own soul memories and names of people, especially those still living, have been changed in order to protect their privacy. The author makes no claim to the veracity of names in past lives.

CONTENTS

Preface

As a child, my favourite stories began with "Once upon a time..." I knew those words would set the scene for a very different world filled with magic, mystery and most of all, transformation. I didn't know then that I would find magic in my own life, much less write about past-life memories.

But can you prove them? I hear you asking. Are they real?

Is proof the only validity in writing a story, I respond.

Dr. Ian Stevenson has compiled significant studies on the possibility of past-lives that are scientifically valid. *Twenty Cases Suggestive of Reincarnation* remains one of the landmark books for those seeking objective proof. For those who discount the very possibility of reincarnation, his book will remain one of life's little mysteries, and cannot be easily dismissed.

My purpose in writing this book is somewhat different. I do not seek to prove the truth of these stories, and indeed, if the reader prefers to dismiss them as complete fiction, that's entirely his, or her, choice.

My hope is that some small aspect of this journey resonates with people everywhere, especially women, regardless of race, colour, education or religious background, for the historic condition of the feminine has largely been one of subjugation and loss. And yet, the feminine principle is creativity, heart and power.

If you are a man reading this, remember the essence of soul experience is equally valid. Even though you may have a male body in this lifetime, you have undoubtedly experienced at least one incarnation as a woman.

I feel fortunate that I have reached a stage in my development where I can remember – and write about – my own past-lives. For in writing my story, I achieve integration and forgiveness on a deeper level, releasing the past and moving into the present experience.

Contrary to popular opinion, regression therapy is not about dwelling in the past. Its very purpose only exists to help us live more fully in the present.

I like to think of regression therapy as a quantum experience, which takes place outside of time and space, for the memory that is triggering the clinical condition is often not found in the current life. One does not need to believe in a former life in order for the treatment to be effective; the efficacy occurs as the person releases the stuck memory or pattern that contributed to the presenting issue.

The main point here, however, is that few people remember their past-lives.

I am not going into minute detail regarding the therapeutic approach as one of my teachers, Dr. Roger Woolger, has written an excellent book on the subject of regression therapy, (*Other Lives, Other Selves*). However, it may be of interest to the reader to know about my background. I am a past-life therapist with a M.Sc. Degree in Consciousness and Transpersonal Psychology. I have witnessed dramatic breakthroughs when people release patterns that no longer serve them.

How did I get here? Well, it has taken me time – in earth years – to fully embrace my inner psychic. We all have sensing or intuitive ability, knowing seconds in advance when the phone will ring or who will be on the other end of the line, for example. We're familiar with the term 'gut feeling'. But in my case, I also knew things before they happened; even as a child, I would know when marriages wouldn't work out, and I would find myself in very deep water when I blurted out my opinion on these matters. Tact was not part of the equation.

I began to break free of my desire for *normality* in my early 20s when I began experiencing unexplained phenomena.

I eventually read everything I could about the spiritual path, what exactly is this path and where does it take us? What is reincarnation? What is karma?

I then began remembering my own past-lives.

These memories initially came to me in dreams, vivid feelings with extraordinary images in cinematic technicolour. I realized then that dreams really are windows to the soul, and over a period of 20 years, I built a bridge between the psychological and the spiritual to better understand both my human and expanded self.

I trained in many disciplines including aromatherapy, hypnosis and psychotherapy before I realized I had to walk a new path in consciousness; I was still searching for a training that would show me the way, rather than find my own direction.

This was not an easy task.

In my case, it was the search for that ideal romantic relationship that made me feel separate. I saw that everyone else was in – or appeared to be in - relationship. I wondered if I was the only woman in my circle of friends who had been celibate for how many years...seven? (Doesn't that make me a born again virgin?)

I wondered if the number seven held a key as I remembered the seven primary chakras, or energy centres.

Could these chakras, associated with the Eastern tradition, be affecting my life in the present? If so, perhaps I was under the influence of a cosmic (and causal) connection, linking my past-lives together in a way I hadn't even imagined until now.

Was this search for love somehow linked to the chakras? Or was I merely unlucky in love?

A very wise spiritual teacher reminded me that in truth, we don't really need to search for love, we simply tune in; it is by the tuning in that we recognize – and remember – the essence and nature of who and what we are.

As I moved more deeply into meditation, I was shown a series of lives which appeared to answer my questions about love. I was told that I would now write about my journey through these lives until I reached my current life, symbolized by my crown chakra. (This adventure will be published in a later book.)

These memories, or memoirs, represent qualities associated with the chakras, while each story continues its distinctive quest for the experience of love.

This, in essence, is my own soul story; the story of six different women, and the way in which each of them influenced me in the here and now.

As I open up to this inner quest and re-experience these powerful past lives, I dedicate this book to the Divine Feminine.

Thank you for taking this journey with me.

Theresa Pugh

Chapter One

1st Chakra - Colour Red

This base chakra is about our connection to the earth and helps us feel grounded in the present. It is linked to issues we have around money and feelings of home, home within ourselves, and being at home on the planet.

As I prepared to walk through this passageway of time, I saw in front of me a swirling red mist. I knew this life would deal with foundational issues relating to security and survival, my place on earth, literally matters of life and death. From a positive perspective, this soul level chakra is about assertiveness, strength of will and courage; on the negative side, the root chakra brings up insecurity, fearfulness and a feeling of self-pity. Would I see this as a good life or as a struggle? And did it matter? I was only told in order to achieve integration on my soul path, I needed to review these lives and learn from the perspective of my experience. I was given the gift of remembering, which is not to be taken lightly. And so I began.

Prologue

Despite my intuitive ability, I like to check in with psychics from time-to-time and see what they have to tell me. When I was 20-something and found myself living in Toronto, a psychic told me about a connection I had with San Francisco. She said that if I waited for love, (and waiting has never been one of my strong points), I would meet the man I would marry. However, she added, if I was impatient, and couldn't wait, (I was only 25 and how many of us are patient at that age?), I would meet an old flame and we would be together for seven years. She turned out to be absolutely correct, and I didn't visit San Francisco for another 20 years.

In 2008, a past-life therapy conference brought me to the Golden Gate city and I happened to meet a man on the airplane who seemed surprisingly familiar. I had the strangest feeling that he and I had met before.

This man from the plane, whom I shall call Jackson, appeared to be an individual of integrity, solid and practical with good follow-through. He says what he means and means what he says. These are increasingly rare characteristics in this day and age and I found his approach to life very refreshing. Although his current occupation is in the financial industry, his previous work, according to my past-life memories, appeared to be as a journalist for one of the Bay area newspapers.

I didn't place him on a pedestal after our meeting and put the brakes on any emerging feelings when he told me he was married. Like that old song: 'I fall in love too easily, I fall in love too fast', my Achilles heel has been the recognition of men from a past-life where I then expect we would simply pick up where we left off. Sadly, these men often have other commitments, where I have remained surprisingly free in this lifetime.

It wasn't until I went through a bizarre personal crisis, as floods of memories poured in, that my old life in the Bay area emerged.   There were good reasons for me not remembering that life, as I was murdered by the age of 24.

Dangerous Liaisons

I had moved to San Francisco from the American mid-west. I had high hopes of being discovered and found the early stages of talking-pictures quite exciting. I seem to recall that I dreamt of becoming a cabaret singer, but how much of that was smoke and puff, I'm not really sure.

I had a pretty good voice, sultry, more of an alto, ideally suited for the new jazz movement that was about to break wide open, but, really, I was a wide-eyed ingénue. That's mostly how I remember myself: In love with the idea of being discovered but not really expecting anything much to happen. Still, I moved out west as soon as I could scrape together the money to pay my way. I don't recall brothers or sisters; if I had family, I must have lost my father in the First World War and my mother remained overseas. There was an Aunt, or a friendly relative of some sort, who had cared for me. I certainly wasn't traumatized by my upbringing but I didn't have a strong sense of belonging either. I wanted to make my own way in the world, be seen and be recognized. I wanted to be Someone with a capital 'S'. I wanted to be brave and daring, set the world on fire, and most of all, I wanted to be loved.

It was nearly spring of 1924 when I packed up a few clothes and headed to California, the sunshine state; where even in the middle of winter, the temperature was lovely and warm, at least by mid-western standards. When Idaho was still covered in snow by early March, California was blooming. There were wild flowers in the desert, and a warmth to the air, which made me feel that I really had stumbled into paradise. I wasn't entirely prepared for the cool fog and mist I uncovered in San Francisco, but it wasn't unpleasant either. I had made up my mind that San Francisco really was the city of dreams; I was convinced it would be my city, my home and here in San Francisco would be where I would make my dreams come true.

I managed to find lodgings in an 1890s boarding house, a pretty Victorian-style building trimmed in blue and white. I found myself sitting around dinner with people from all walks of life, most of them older than me, some widowed, others in transition. A motherly looking woman called Pearl took me under her wing and suggested I meet some of her friends who worked at a local café in Sausalito. "You never know who you might meet," she said to me, "especially a young girl like yourself. One day the man of your dreams might just walk through that door and into your heart. Life happens like that. Sudden-like when you're least expecting it, your whole world changes."

Naturally I asked her if that is how things happened for her.

"Oh," she said. "I always knew Howard and I would end up together. We went to the same Sunday school, knew each other since we were babies. We married at 18 and had nearly ten years together before he went off to war. The influenza took him. I miss him every day. But I'm luckier than most. At least we had our time together, I can't ask for anything more."

My attention was drawn away by the owner of the boarding house, Mrs. Grenadier. She had also lost her husband, to the attentions of another woman though, not the war.

"Mary-Anne dear, you must know we have very strict rules here in my establishment. No drinking on the premises and no men in your room. Either offense is an immediate eviction."

The other boarders whispered to each other at her pronouncement. They had heard this story many times before and knew the boarding house owner liked nothing better than to lay down the law in her own house.

"This city is becoming wicked and licentious. I run a respectable establishment here and I am not about to lose my livelihood due to bad behaviour from my boarders. You will see the house is divided up and the quarters for men and women are kept quite separately on different floors. The men have no reason whatsoever, *ever,* to go to the top floors."

She glared at the men around the table and they nodded in acknowledgement.

"They know this. As extra security, you have been given your own key. But do come to me dear if I can help you with anything. You will need someone looking out for you in the city." With that, Mrs. Grenadier proceeded to quarter and spear her potato.

I tried to think of a response when Pearl jumped to my rescue.

"Mrs. Grenadier as I have a niece who is just 18, I will make sure Mary-Anne is introduced to decent people. It's not easy coming to a new city. We all know this. "

"Very well, then. Just make sure she doesn't bring any riff-raff back. I can't have lovesick boys lowering the tone of my establishment. Now if you'll excuse me, I will check on the tea." With that, Mrs. Grenadier flounced off to take dominion over her kitchen.

A low hum of conversation erupted around the table. The people sitting across from me certainly appeared to epitomize respectability. A teacher, a writer, a couple making their way up the west coast to Canada...I really couldn't imagine any low life breaking through the impenetrable shield established by the owner of this boarding house, and that thought in itself gave me some comfort as I began to make plans later that night for my new life.

The next morning I accompanied Pearl to her café. This included the additional excitement of a short boat ride to the town of Sausalito. Although Pearl didn't consider herself better than any of the others who worked for her, she was, in fact, the owner of the business which she had established with her husband 11 years earlier. I told Pearl that I really wanted to break into cabaret singing but I dare not tell that to Mrs. Grenadier as she would no doubt consider night clubs the lowest form of licentiousness, along with prostitution and alcohol.

Pearl was thoughtful with her response. "It's not impossible," she said, "especially as San Francisco is becoming more of a big city. I think there are places you could sing. But I don't know about the people who run them. That's what we'll have to watch for – gangsters and the like. Money-laundering is becoming a big deal – attracts those mafia families - you know where businesses are a front for shady deals. Especially in Sausalito. You don't want to go and get mixed up with something like that now. That would not do at all."

With that pronouncement, she swept me into the café and introduced me to her extended family. There was Jimmy the bus boy, Sarah, Peony and Eliza who covered most of the waitressing, Theo the cook, and his assistant Dino. As Eliza had to leave in the afternoon to care for her elderly mother, Pearl asked me if I would like to help out. Although I had not worked as a waitress before, it seemed like a perfectly reasonable way to earn a living while I figured out how to launch my new career. Life continued in this way for the next year or so, pleasant enough but not entirely fulfilling either.

The following spring as April rolled into May, a young man called Billy Walker strolled into the café and asked for Pearl. It seemed he worked for the Sausalito paper and wanted to write a story on a local hero. As her husband, Howard, was born in the area, grew up in the town, and gave up his life for his country, he fit the bill in every respect. He was the quintessential small-town boy who sacrificed for his country. He embodied the values of small-town America and Pearl, in her own way, was quite a legend herself. Her small café was renowned for its home cooking and she had a decency and broadmindedness that had somehow stayed intact despite the loss of her husband. She kept him alive in her heart, but didn't lose her heart, and that balancing act was a rare accomplishment.

I ended up chatting to Billy after he wrote the story, or perhaps I should say he hung around with his soft drink, after he interviewed Pearl.

I told him I was fairly new in town and was looking for my big break. He seemed to take this all in with a grain of salt, didn't think I was strange or anything, which was something of a relief when I really didn't have anything to show for myself. I wondered if he knew people on the paper – entertainment correspondents perhaps who could point me in the right direction. I really didn't even know where to start. After all, I said to him, I couldn't very well just walk into a nightclub and ask for an audition, could I. That would take a brazenness which I really didn't possess.

"Why not?" he said. "How do you think people get started? Gotta start somewhere."

"Well, what about you? Did you just waltz into the newspaper and demand a job?"

"Not exactly," he replied looking a bit sheepish. "I had an Uncle who knew someone on the news desk. Working on the paper has always, always, always been my dream, so I began helping out over the summer, you know when I was still in school."

I looked at him again. He really didn't look much older than 20.

"I know I look young for my age, but I've been on the paper for three years now, since high school. I'm 21. I also wanted that big break, hard hitting news and everything. So far, I've been doing the soft stuff, local news, obits, taking a few photos; not exactly Pulitzer prize winning material, that's really what I want. Action. You know?"

I knew. I could relate to his ambition and drive. He seemed like a nice boy, freckles, sandy-blonde hair, not too tall, almost plump. He said his parents lived locally and he had never been away from home. The Bay area was his life; he hadn't even dreamed of moving to another city.

"Why bother," he said, "when everything I could ever want or need is right here in front of me. No point in chasing after things, if it's meant to be, it'll come to me. That's the way life works. Simple."

I wondered at his easy logic. So straightforward. Admirable really. My dreams were so much grander, bigger and more complicated than his desire to simply be known for his work.

"Take you for instance," he said. "Here I come into the café to interview Pearl for a story. My editor sent me. And here you are – a really great girl."

"Say, would you like to go out with me Saturday? There's a new show on, we could meet for a soda afterwards, what do you say?"

His offer was so sincere and heartfelt there really wasn't any reason to say no. Although I still didn't know how I would become a singer, I thought maybe, just maybe, I would land a boyfriend. Now that was progress of a different sort.

Pearl was delighted with my news but told me to keep it to myself. "Even if it is completely innocent and you just get to know this boy, nothing serious, if you know what I mean, Mrs. Grenadier will be watching you like a hawk. And if it does become serious and you two marry, then you won't need to live under her roof anymore, if you see what I mean."

I did and agreed with her logic. Better keep these things to myself, at least until I knew which direction I was heading.

As it turned out, we had a marvelous time together that Saturday afternoon. Billy or Billy-Bob as he was often called, (due to his middle name being Robert), was good fun. He wasn't my idea of the perfect man by any stretch of the imagination as my mind pictured a dark-haired, lean and well-dressed man, someone sophisticated and daring, rather like a World War 1 fighter pilot, whereas Billy was ordinary in a nice, kind sort of way. But he was also solid and practical, he knew what he wanted from life and I had the feeling that he would achieve his dream, especially as he had a way of making people talk. I didn't open up that easily and didn't think anyone would find my life story even a tiny bit interesting. But Billy kept asking me questions 'til he had ferreted out of me every last bit of information: what I liked and didn't like, where I grew up, what I liked doing, my favourite authors and even my first memory at the age of two. He said hardly anyone remembers anything before the age of three, or even four, so the fact I remember something at the age of two made me unique. I guess Billy's special gift was making other people feel good..

Over that summer, Pearl said she never saw me looking happier and I had to agree. Although I never thought my looks were anything special, (I had wavy hair at a time most girls were wearing short, straight hair), and I thought my face too long and pointy. I really wanted a nice heart-shape like the silent screen star Clara Bow, but Pearl said I had a shine to me like a new penny. She figured this was due entirely to Billy, and Billy, of course, said the same thing. By that autumn we were officially an item and Billy had asked me to marry him. We agreed on a long engagement of a year or two as we really didn't have a dime between us. We hoped to use that time to save enough money so we could afford a nice wedding.

I settled into life at the café and quite enjoyed meeting all the regulars. I still had a hankering to prove myself though, especially now that I'd be settling down with Billy. I didn't think it would be quite appropriate to sing in a nightclub once I was married and determined to find some way to live a little before the big day. I ended up badgering Billy to take me 'round to some of the nightclubs, even if they were seedy, I was 21 years of age now and could cope with a crowd of people who weren't 'so nice'. That's what he always said: 'Those places aren't so nice'. I ended up telling him that I didn't want to dine with these people, I saw people every day at the café, most of whom were 'very nice' indeed, I said to Billy I just wanted to get in through the door so someone, somewhere, could hear me sing.

As luck would have it, Billy's editor finally gave him a reason to explore the music scene. There was a new sensation in town, someone from New York who was pulling in crowds like nobody's business. He had an Italian background which immediately led to rumours of a mafia connection.

How else, people whispered, could this new kid, not much older than 23, be such a big sensation? He hadn't really established himself, but by all accounts still received top billing everywhere he went. He must have backers in powerful places. Billy told me this story could be his chance to break into the big time. If he could find one shred of evidence that linked this rising star to the big crime families, the police chief, William Quinn himself would take action. He had no tolerance for eastern gangsters at all.

Although San Francisco largely tolerated drinking in the prohibition years, neither the mayor or the police chief wanted lingering memories of the gold rush era, which was something of a hey-day for prostitution and gambling. Although other American cities may put up with crime families, San Francisco would be different: clean and safe, a liberal utopia for people from around the world. I said to Billy this was a big vision for one city to create; besides, how could anyone know that people would come from all over the world? Isn't San Francisco sort of out of the way for people from all around the world? If they lived in Asia or England, it would take weeks and weeks to get here.

Billy didn't tell me that San Francisco was already a port town or the clear fact that the city already boasted the largest Chinatown in America. No, Billy wasn't so mundane. He simply told me: "Large oak trees spring from tiny acorns." That's the thing about Billy. He always had the perfect answer for the thorniest problems.

The next night we found ourselves in Club Rouge, a tiny hole-in-the-wall establishment not far from

Market Street. Some people called it a Speak Easy, there were dozens in the area, but this presumably was the place picked out for the launch of the amazing singer. Billy told me at the time that I should just keep my head down, and not say anything as it probably wasn't the right time to draw attention to myself as he was trying to crack open the news story of the decade. I agreed to bide my time and took an active, if quiet, interest in my environment. There were soft drinks available at the front of the establishment and lots of wooden chairs and small tables. Billy said the bathtub gin was probably in the back and we didn't need to worry about that as our assignment really centred on observing the people who had come to watch the singer. And the singer himself, whose name I am not at liberty to disclose.

At any rate, the evening took my breath away due entirely to the appearance of said singer. The man looked as though he had quite literally walked out of the pages of my imagination and into this quirky little saloon. He was lanky in build, with a face that could only be sculptured by a master craftsman, high cheekbones and piercing blue eyes. The man was beautiful beyond my wildest dreams and if Billy thought he had some competition that night, he was too wise to point out the obvious. Of course I knew that men like that did not fall for girls like me, besides this singer could have the pick of any girl in the world; I would stick to Billy like glue through thick and thin, but girls were allowed to dream, weren't they?

Billy said he wanted to see evidence of other Italian people at the joint that night, people who could conceivably be part of the mafia. But we just saw the usual crowd, people who looked to be typical locals, certainly nothing out of the ordinary. We couldn't find out why that particular club was selected to launch the debut of this rising sensation but Billy thought money had changed hands, there had to be some reason, he said, regarding the venue. Clearly we needed to put a better plan into action and this is where Billy enlisted my help.

He asked me if I would mind acting as a decoy, perhaps gain information from the singer, and as I genuinely wanted to pursue a career in that field, why not?

Little did Billy know, (or perhaps he did), that my eyes were way beyond infatuation when it came to this man; I figured there was nothing I wouldn't do to get his attention, although to be honest, I didn't have a very good idea of where the line would be between nothing and anything.

At the end of his set, I approached the young singer and told him how much I loved his voice.

He looked at me in a bemused sort of way: "Is that so," he said? "What do you like about it?"

"Well," I stumbled, momentarily surprised at his question. "You actually; it's you that I like." I realized that my face had begun to turn a rather unattractive shade of a nearly ripe strawberry as the blush spread up my neck.

To my surprise, he grinned at my discomfort. "That's honest," he said. "I like that in a girl. Tell you what, I'm playing at the big hall tomorrow night, come meet me after the show – tell them Ricky sent you. They'll let you in and give you the best seats in the house – you and your boyfriend."

I nodded at him not believing my luck. "Thank you," I said. "Thank you so much. We'll be there."

I couldn't wait to tell Billy the good news – we were in at the big gig tomorrow. Now that felt like progress.

When we arrived at the hall the next night, as requested, I said: "Ricky sent me." To my surprise, the doorman nodded and took my arm, leaving Billy standing at the door. I turned to see if Billy would follow behind me but he told me to go on ahead. It looked as though there was only room for one that night.

The bodyguard escorted me to a private box facing the stage, telling me that the singer would see me backstage at the end of the evening. I began to feel a little worried about this picture. After all, I had expected Billy to come in to the concert hall with me; I wondered if this decoy business was as harmless as we thought? I determined that I would sneak away to the stage door after the first number and see if there wasn't some way to get Billy into the box with me. I was sure he would wait for me out back as I knew there was no way he would leave me in the lurch, especially as I was on assignment for him.

After the first number finished, I had to sit through a couple more songs before I felt comfortable enough to leave my seat. I made my way around the back of the auditorium groping my way in the dark to what seemed to be a set of stairs leading onto the main street. Perhaps I could use this exit to reach the street level. I didn't think I should draw attention to myself especially as Billy was denied entry. Something about this situation didn't make sense to me: initially there were meant to be seats reserved for both of us, now I was the only one allowed access.

I very quietly opened the door and heard it thud behind me. The stairwell itself was pitch black, I couldn't see behind me or in front of me but figured if I kept walking down the stairs, I would eventually find the way out. As I reached the landing, my eyes began to acclimatize to the lack of light and I saw another door off to my right. Perhaps that would take me to the dressing room area. As I still wasn't entirely sure where the steps were taking me, I thought it best if I found someone to ask, perhaps there was a helpful soul in the green room who could tell me how to get out the back way.

The next door I opened led to a small chamber with a boiler at the far end. That didn't seem to be the way out, so perhaps I was wrong about the back stage area. Maybe it was on an entirely different level and I should be walking up the stairs, rather than down. By this time, my heart was beginning to beat rather fast and I wondered if

I should just find my way back to the box-seat. Maybe it didn't matter whether or not Billy was with me, I was fully capable of speaking to the singer myself after the show; surely he wouldn't do anything to me, would he? With all those girls at his disposal, I was sure the singer was simply displaying a certain generosity to a star-struck girl such as me. Still, I would feel better if Billy were with me, in which case my mind reasoned, we would be up in the box, not stuck down here in this endless corridor. As my feet began to climb the staircase again, I thought I heard someone behind me. But no, that would be impossible. No one had followed me down, I would have heard them. Surely, I was alone in here and the sound was simply my overactive imagination. I paused. Nothing.

I continued my upward climb feeling confident that I didn't have more than another twenty stairs to go before I reached my original destination.

I didn't make it. I realized too late that someone in the stairwell was intent on taking my life. As I left my body and moved towards the light, I saw myself lying strangled on that cold, cement floor. All my dreams, all that young life, snuffed out. Mostly I was worried about Billy. I didn't want him to blame himself.

My ambition as much as his, placed me in that unenviable situation: survival of the fittest on planet earth. I was murdered as a warning...Billy had ambition and wanted to break open the story, but it didn't work out that way; he didn't get the story and he lost the girl. I dreamt of fame but mostly I wanted love.

The base chakra speaks of survival, being grounded and the practicalities of life. That seemed to be the key message from that lifetime. I had my head in the clouds, full of personal ambition and ego. I wasn't a bad person, merely unaware. I found love but I didn't hang on to it... I wonder what soul lessons I'll learn from the next life. Will I be any wiser?

Chapter Two

2nd Chakra - Colour Orange

This chakra relates to sexuality, self respect and creativity. With a well-balanced chakra we have the ability to give and receive within our relationships while still respecting our own boundaries.

Balanced: Creativity, joy, aliveness.

Out-of-balance: Destructive, depressed.

Courtesan in the French Court

1775: Palace of Versailles

I see myself dressed in the finest of gowns, shimmering blue satin, so low-cut that my breasts are all but exposed; my face is powdered, a beautiful looking face with dancing, violet blue eyes, mischievous and naughty: I am wearing a powdered wig that was also the fashion of the day. Around my throat sits a wide diamond necklace.

Sexual intrigue was part of the game; I gave myself willingly to nearly any man in a position of power. Sometimes he gave me jewels, at other times there would be an exchange of information and he would let something slip, (and I let something slip); and that piece of gossip or strategy, (should he be a military man), went straight to the King's men. I didn't know the Queen Marie Antoinette, she was considered cold, aloof even, by many of us but then again, she didn't need to talk to me, (although it may have helped her to have had more friends at the court);

and yet I respected her accomplishment. Although she was a Royal by birth, and by all accounts determined to capture her King, it was largely agreed that she had risen to her place as Queen consort of France through beauty, wit and guile, qualities that remain essential in any French woman. I should know.

She wasn't so different to me and many others like us: we were all a commodity and had our price; even those of us who were considered a treasure, a jewel, sometimes full of luster, other times hidden away in the closet; we still had our price, and we knew it. The entire society was artificial, like the icing on a cake. But even the mixture of icing and sugar when set, held the body of the cake together in a way which couldn't easily be broken. So that is the way it was at the French Court before the Revolution, and the way it was with me, until it was no more.

I was 26 years old when I died at the hands of a jealous lover, and his jealousy came as a surprise to me: I thought he knew the rules of the game:

first and foremost: it was only a game. Like the toss of a dice, gambling was a popular past-time at the palace: some days there were winners, other days there were losers. It wasn't really a serious business: gambling, whoring, and drinking: it made the world go 'round, nothing more, nothing less. And yet this game lost me my life. I was devastated.

But let me backtrack to the main event: the purpose of that life.

For me that life was frivolous. Should I have felt shame that I chose the path of courtesan? No. Not in 18th century France; not at that time, in that place. For some people, those of us lucky enough to find it, and not lose our head, the era was a gay time, full of riotous living – and loving. It was a time of excess in every way.

I was, some would say, (and a few did), an opportunist: I had assets and I used them. By the age of 15, I had caught the eye of a gentleman's gentleman, a person of sufficient pull to allow me to gain entrance to Versailles and from that place, I was able to enter into an arranged marriage which, shall I say, made it very expedient for us both, especially as his sexual proclivities were not with the fairer sex. Nevertheless, his marriage to a young, beautiful girl with a good-enough bloodline and background created the entrée to society that he desired and I deserved. If my occupation wasn't the most genteel, there certainly wasn't anyone at the court who could judge me: everyone was at it with everyone else. From this perspective, I saw that I was in the right place at the right time: I was able to collect a reasonable nest-egg to put aside when my skin began to sag and the men required younger girls. I suspected that time was not far off when I met the dashing Henri.

Henri was not world-weary like so many of the others; he had a zest for life, which I found almost refreshing; had I begun to suspect that he really was in love with me, I would have broken it off much sooner than I did, but I didn't really imagine that men fell in love with courtesans anymore. He knew what I was. Or at least I thought he did. Certainly, I was attached to the court, as was he, but looking back at this now, could he have misread the signs? I loved him as a man, of course, how could I not? He was charming and virile, attractive and cultured. It was said he was a distant cousin to the King of Spain, and finding oneself able to seek refuge in another country should the unthinkable happen was always a good policy. But love him? Certainly not. Did he really imagine that I, Countess X, would give up my position and everything I had worked for to run away with him? Surely even young men could not be so naive but this assertion, proved my undoing.

He saw me in the arms of another man, in my bedchamber, while I was in the throws of orgasm; he knew it was me and called out. I could hardly pull away and pretend that what he saw was not what he saw: it was what it was. I was making love to another man. I heard him say my name as he left the room sounding for all the world like a love-sick puppy. Surely he wouldn't do anything rash: his whole life was before him. I pulled away as quickly as I could and said: "Henri, un moment, s'il vous plait. It is nothing."

My paramour of the moment had already turned over and gone to sleep. I was certainly not worthy of his lingering attention, but Henri, Henri was another matter. I couldn't understand what he was doing in my chamber at this time; we had an understanding that we saw each other much later in the day, after dinner, and now, the time was not yet eight.

I pulled on a shift around my shoulders and hurried to the balcony to look for Henri. I saw him attempting to climb over the railing and tried to pull him back. We struggled. He was very cold, as though the light and heat had left his body. Suddenly, our combined weight snapped the fragile railing and we fell to our deaths.

As I tuned in to the memories and feelings of the Countess, I knew I was accessing the 2nd chakra.

It was a life where I lived and loved much. Perhaps I was not as emotionally sensitive to the needs of others as I could have been, but after all, what does one expect from a courtesan? She is giving her body in the sexual act but not sharing her heart. Henri had asked too much of me in that lifetime. Although I didn't know it then, he was in love with me; and in that final moment when he realized what I was, his own zest for life was extinguished. Henri, it seems, was not a great pretender, and really had no place in the French Court. But that is another story for another time.

This life was about sexuality and creativity and the negative aspects of this chakra were destruction and despondency. It seemed that I had experienced both sides of the coin. My sexuality as the Countess was very vibrant indeed; I didn't feel as though I had any lingering doubts about my occupation, to the contrary, I fully embraced the mood of the time believing that I had found my right place in the world. I suppose one could say that was also a creative approach to life: making full use of my assets. In retrospect, Henri may have done me a favour by his jealousy. I may not have had so much to live for within a few years;

not only would my body sag and looks fade, the French Revolution was just around the corner by which time, I suspect, real friends were few and far between, especially in the French Court.

I wondered to what extent that existence influenced my years of celibacy in my current incarnation?

Perhaps this was simply a karmic rebalancing. As I was very licentious in that life, perhaps I would need to abstain. (This life perhaps?)

For starters, I now take sexual relationships very seriously, and friends tell me 'too seriously' as it took me a decade to recover from my first love affair. Perhaps that was the karmic outcome from that life as the Countess.

I will have to see what my other lives reveal to me.

Chapter Three

3rd *Chakra - Colour Yellow*

This is the area of the personality, the ego and the intellect. The solar plexus chakra deals with issues of self worth; how we feel about ourselves and others.

Balanced: Feelings of confidence, alertness, optimism and good-humour.

Out-of-balance: Feelings of inferiority, overly analytical, sarcastic, pessimistic.

Denial of the Self: the Duty of Marriage

I sat there silently facing the window but not seeing. I didn't see the beauty of the autumn day. I didn't feel the crisp coolness as the weather began to turn or hear the sound of the chestnuts dropping to the ground. I saw nothing except his face as he left the room: the face that would haunt me until I drew my last breath.

I knew this parting would end my life as I knew it, and my life would never be the same again; I would never be the same again even though I would look the same to the outside world. I would continue on as generations of women had done before me, and would do again, for the sake of duty.

For the sake of duty. Duty. Such a loaded word. Why do we prize duty above our heart's truth?

Why was I locked into this rigid life? I might as well wear a straitjacket for all the freedom of expression I possessed.   Is a woman born free? No, surely not.

I am my father's chattel: Expected to marry a man chosen for his bloodline as I am matched for mine.

We Englishwomen are little better than breeding stock; no, make it *less* than breeding stock, for horses are treated with more dignity and respect than women such as I.   Any idea of freedom is folly itself, and cuts against the grain of polite society.   Horses, I believe, are held in greater esteem and perhaps didn't risk their hearts as I had done.

I realized in that moment that purchasing the finest silks and cloths are of small consequence if the company surrounding one is less than agreeable.

And yet, what irony, that I am slave to wealth. That by refusing to marry the appointed squire, I would (as part of the great love given me by my father, or so he said) be completely cut-off, not only shunned by polite society with every door closed to me, but no longer having even the comfort of a bed and a roof over my head. And all for my own good. Or so said my father. My mother, of course, had no opinion on this matter being "merely a woman" and also subjected to an 'arranged marriage' which she told me in a private moment had worked out rather better than anticipated.

So, yes, with all this apparent wealth, I am no more secure, perhaps less so, than a scullery maid. She may not have two shillings to her name but more often than not, her services are required by the likes of my mother for the duration of her life. She knows her place and pecking order; perhaps then, she and I are equals. Perhaps I do *not* know my place in the scheme of things and believed, quite wrongly, (as I have now discovered), that love does not conquer all.

The love of my heart, Andrew James Fraser, is not a common man. He was simply not the preferred choice. His family owned sufficient land to be called gentlemen farmers. Andrew himself joined the navy as he didn't like the other alternatives available to him: medicine or the ministry. I think I fell in love with him the moment we met – over three years ago now. I was only 16 and he was a little older. As we had acquaintances in common, my parents didn't immediately discourage the friendship, but when he joined the navy, they saw trouble. Still as they realized there was nothing more substantial than the odd letter going back and forth, they didn't immediately put an end to this union; they certainly did *not* expect a grand passion. Nor did they anticipate that I would flatly refuse to marry the man chosen for me. I had no interest in marrying another. Andrew was the man my heart desired. How could it be any other way? The mistake I made, if it was my mistake to make, was my misunderstanding of my place in society. Although I knew my family was in a privileged position, it didn't dawn on me that this privilege was maintained through the duty of marriage. I assumed that a young man introduced to me by a family friend would be quite worthy of my hand in marriage. I certainly felt he was my equal. He embodied the qualities my heart desired: tenderness and daring, loyalty and devotion. I didn't believe that another man more worthy of my love could exist in all of England.

But one day it all changed. On my 18th birthday I was brought to our very best room reserved for special guests and introduced to Sir Charles Elliott Black. He had to be at least 40 years of age and possessed social connections at every level. In addition to owning half the county, he was on personal terms with the Royal Family; some believed he wanted to marry into the Family but it was said he would have no one other than my self. I didn't know why he was so set on marrying me. I'm sure I wasn't considered a great beauty and I certainly had strong opinions, which were considered entirely unsuitable for a young lady. Be that as it may, he wanted me, and only I would do. However, he also wanted me to come to him of my own volition and I found this exceedingly strange. It seemed he wanted me to love him. Perhaps he wanted to brag that a woman half his age only had eyes for him, but I was simply unaware that men could be so vain. Surely that was a woman's prerogative?

And so it was that I found myself sitting at my window feeling nothing, seeing nothing, but the face of my one true love.

I was told that unless I made it clear to him that I could never see him again I would be cut-off.

And I considered that possibility at some length. To be cut off, almost ex-communicated from both my family and society would not really be a bad thing, except that I would have no means of survival. No means at all. I was completely unfit to take up any sort of employment and wouldn't be hired in London even if I were. I could hardly run off with Andrew as he was stationed for years at a time with the Royal Navy; when he was off at sea, what would happen to me? Besides, he didn't want a penniless outcast for a wife. The scandal of my very name would probably put an end to his career with the Navy and then what would he do?

It was a nightmare: Completely impossible and absolutely impractical. I had no choice but to accept the terms and conditions of this marriage. I was little better than a chattel; a term which I would come to loathe over time.

And so it was when Andrew called on his next furlough home, he found me in a very different frame of mind than anticipated. He had hoped, it seemed, that our engagement could be discussed; he wanted to ask my father for my hand in marriage. Unfortunately, I was now engaged to quite a different sort of man who would brook no competition.

I heard the sound of horses' hooves long before Andrew arrived at the door. As a special boon, I had requested a private meeting with him in the front sitting room, and knew that even if ears were pressed against the wall, at least we had the appearance of privacy, and for that, at least, I was thankful.

As he was ushered into the small green room, I steeled myself.   I didn't consider myself much of an actress: I wore my heart on my sleeve and spoke my mind to all and sundry, but in this moment, I had to find the resolve within myself to put on the performance of a lifetime. I had to demonstrate to him that I no longer loved him in such a way that he would find this not only believable but credible.   It was critical to his future. I no longer cared about myself, but I wouldn't have his future ruined for something that was not his fault.

"Andrew," I said as I turned around to face him, "How good of you to come."

I held out my hand in the air as I motioned him to stay silent for a moment.

"I have some news for you, which I must say quickly and send you on your way. I am engaged to be married and I can't see you again. This engagement is made with my full consent and blessing. As a married woman, it would not be appropriate to remain in contact as my husband is to be Sir Charles. I believe you know of him?"

Andrew was shocked into a speechless silence.

"Yes, of course but, but...he's over 40 years of age. When did this happen?"

"The details are not important. Suffice to say this union is important to me and my family. I hope you understand."

Silence.

"Good-bye then."

"Good-bye!" Andrew stormed towards me. "But this is preposterous. Absolute...rubbish. Isabel...you don't, you can't love this man...we...we have an understanding...you know how much I love you...don't you?"

"There is nothing more to be said on this matter. I really must wish you good-day now."

"No! Isabel, look at me. Look me in the eyes and tell me you don't love me. Look me in the eyes and tell me you want to marry this, this other person and not me. Say it!"

My back was turned to him. I swallowed. Could I find the strength, the resolve, to carry out this one final request? Could I live with myself knowing this memory would stay with me – and him – forever? Did I have a choice?

I slowly turned towards him and looked him straight in the eyes, peering into the depths of his being. "I don't love you. I never did. Can't you understand that? Now will you please leave us in peace?"

He said nothing to me as he turned to leave. Simply looked at me, in me, and through me. And left. Silence filled the air.

The silence that would haunt me forever.

As I lay on my death bed years later, I acknowledged that I had made it to old age. My five children were there with me; Charles had passed away some years earlier after succumbing to a bronchial infection. The age difference didn't prove much of a problem. We did our own thing: he with the men, me, raising the family. As generations of woman had before me and would again after me, I performed my duty to perfection. I became known as the perfect hostess, the perfect wife and the perfect mother. Upon marrying Charles, I was elevated to the position of Lady, which was a title my mother had wanted for herself and she achieved this vicariously through me. There wasn't a day when I wasn't the envy of someone in society for I was widely known as the woman who had it all. Charles doted on me in his own way; and my children were bright and handsome. I didn't want for any material comfort and no door was ever closed to me.

However, as I lay on my death bed at the age of 72, I knew my entire life had been a charade. Yes, there was the appearance of perfection in my life but it was not perfect. I had lost my heart the day Andrew walked out that door. More than my heart, my soul had left, too.

I smiled and nodded throughout that life in deference to society's demands. My father felt relieved that I had finally settled down; I was no longer the willful young girl. I believe he truly felt vindicated regarding my marriage as it was widely considered a brilliant match. Or perhaps he didn't give it a second thought. Certainly no hint of scandal ever touched our door. I never heard from Andrew again, and for all practical purposes, he appeared to have completely disappeared.

The only thing I knew as I lay dying is that I never forgot that moment when I sent him away, for in that choice I took my own life as surely as placing a gun to my head.

From that day forward, I didn't feel again. I didn't feel the love of my husband or the joy of my children.

From that day forward, I became a spectator in my own life peering through a glass darkly, incapable of feeling, numb in my core.

I did my duty in that life but had no love to give, for I died the day I sent away my heart.

My children didn't know a mother's love but they didn't want for anything. They had their place in society. That is all they could ask of me.

Reflecting on that life, I clearly saw the way in which I had been impacted throughout time. In my 21st century life, I know the difference between love and duty.

If there is one lesson I learned from this life, it is the artificial nature of duty imposed upon us by the dictates of society. Duty is not love, although we may choose to carry out particular obligations because we love others, duty imposed upon us for its own sake can never create feelings of personal balance and self-esteem.

There were limitations in that life, despite the material trappings. Perhaps that is why I came into my current life as an orphan? Without strong family roots, I could only rely on myself – and the unseen world. I wasn't beholden to any person, place or thing.

Lack of self-worth and feelings of inferiority have remained with me in this life, and yes, I have felt numb, almost frozen in grief, which suggests to me that I have lived such a life as Isabel.

It is a humbling experience to know that one can live a life of material luxury and not be free to enjoy it; and even worse is my remembrance of that excruciating grief, which had nowhere to go. There is a point beyond heartbreak where we no longer feel.

I wondered if I would ever recapture that sense of aliveness I had lost as a young woman. By remembering this past-life could I put those old ghosts to rest?

Could I forgive everyone associated with that era and reclaim my heart? Awareness, they say, is the first crucial step to healing; perhaps I could learn to love again in my next life.

Chapter Four

4th Chakra - Colour Green

The heart chakra represents the quality of love, being able to give and receive love, joy and well-being.

Balanced: Compassion, generosity, harmony, love.

Out-of-Balance: Indifference, jealousy, miserly, bitterness.

Get Thee to a Nunnery

I didn't know my mother. Ever. I wasn't convinced I was born to a woman and half thought I must be a changeling, delivered by the fairies, or some other magical creature. I must have arrived in the usual way as there wasn't any evidence to the contrary, but to all practical purposes, (apart from my very existence, of course), she didn't exist.

My father was a good man though. Quite kind-hearted, a little aloof perhaps, but I thought that was due to his work. He was a classical scholar and could recite the ancient works by heart: Homer, Plato, and Herodotus, among others; and at a time when woman were rarely educated, I was permitted to sit in on his classes. I studied Latin and understood astronomy; by the age of 12, I could hold my own in a group debate: I could think logically and reason as well as any man. Still, somewhere within me beat the heart of a woman for I adored my father and hoped that one day I could meet and marry a man just like him.

But marriage was the furthest thing from my father's mind. The life of the mind is infinite in its capacity and demands full commitment said my father. I assumed this was why I didn't have a mother; he was already wed to another.

Still, life was pleasant enough. I did what I wanted, which was simply studying with my father. I didn't have to worry about any of those tedious womanly chores such as needlepoint or fancy stitching. If the truth be known, I really couldn't sew a stitch; I didn't have anyone to teach me, although my father showed me the basics of cooking; that was something I rather enjoyed: it was more creative than sticking a thread through a needle, an occupation which to me epitomized the height of boredom in every conceivable way.

But my idyllic life would change sooner than I knew. As I was approaching my 16th birthday, my father told me that he had landed a rather good teaching job at Cambridge, and he would be living within those hallowed halls. As luck would have it, he said he had also found the perfect position for me. As I was growing up, (we never did talk about what I would do as I assumed I would also teach students as he did), he realized that he had failed in his duties towards raising a daughter. I wasn't ready, he suddenly said with some embarrassment, to take my place in society as a young lady; he had been so caught up with intellectual pursuits that he rather belatedly realized he had raised me without due diligence to my gender. I wasn't entirely sure where he was going with this, but his solution, whatever it may be, didn't sound the least bit appealing. As far as I was concerned, I didn't need – or wish to learn – all those airs and graces of being a lady - all a mystery to me. What did I care as long as I had my beloved poets and philosophers? But on the matter of my future, he was adamant.

He took my hand and said: "This is what we must do. I have never spoken of your mother for reasons that I can't share with you at this time. Nevertheless, she had a sister who now has a daughter quite close to your own age. I have arranged for you to stay with them and be a companion to the daughter, Sarah."

He looked at my stubborn face. "It is time Guinevere for you to become a lady. As much as I would like this life together to continue for us, times are changing. Pupils are no longer coming to me, and we must eat. As I cannot take you with me, I have found what I am sure will be an excellent solution. Within a year or two, you will marry and forget all about your old scholar. You'll see."

My father had, in his own way, given my future a great deal of consideration and did what he truly believed was best for me. Even I, with my reluctance to be parted from him, could tell that money was becoming scarce and we could barely afford our lodgings.

And so it was that I was sent to Haddington Hall.

The grounds were beautiful; a 100-acre estate set in parkland with young trees and an enormous expanse of open fields surrounded a gothic looking house. Haddington was renowned in the area as the finest architectural example of its kind, but I found the house somewhat spooky. There were too many turrets for my taste; so many rooms for too few people. Although my mind wasn't given to fevered imaginings as I had a more practical bent, I seemed to sense a menancing presence in the very corridors of the house. I wondered if my father had ever been there. I couldn't believe he would condone the waste of space: twenty, thirty rooms for what – three people? My Aunt's husband had died some years ago and left her comfortable enough, at least from a financial perspective; but in addition to the butler and cook, along with a crew of house-maids and gardeners, the only other inhabitant of the house was Sarah. It seemed a little...excessive.

At first they were courteous to me, eyeing me in a way that could only be described as curious; in a way a dog eyes a bone it can't quite reach. I suppose my father was correct: I was considered an oddity; compared to Sarah, I really didn't have any social graces: she could play the piano forte, sketch and sing; music more than anything appeared to be her main accomplishment, while I was entirely, it seemed, tone deaf. My father wasn't a religious man, so even basic hymns were something of a mystery to me. And there were so many rules and regulations: woman couldn't dress in a certain way later in the day; clothes needed to be changed three times a day: a new ensemble was suddenly required for morning, afternoon and evening; I had brought very few personal belongings with me; a few books and a cloak or two comprised my personal necessities, and now I found myself constantly borrowing Sarah's clothes. We were so similar in age and size that we could have been mistaken for each other; yet our personalities were very different. Although I was widely-read and Sarah didn't admit to ever opening a book, she seemed genuinely pleased at my presence in the household. She confided in me that she had never really believed in my existence as my mother hadn't been seen for 16 years, so the idea of a cousin lurking out there in the world had come as a tremendous surprise, but not, she said, an entirely unwelcome one.

The months went by and spring turned to summer. I began to meet the neighbouring families who were comprised of the typical clergy, land-owners and a small class of merchants. All the young men, it seemed, were either away at sea or defending the honour of Great Britain in far-flung places such as Africa. Sarah had trouble understanding why I preferred reading a book to attending a tea-dance, but I told her that I didn't think I would ever learn to dance as she could and found the whole affair more trouble than it was worth. Despite my protestations, she insisted I attend an event with her on the afternoon of the 25th of July.

The day was sunny enough, which meant our walk through the village of Haddington did not harm our shoes or cause us the least bit of inconvenience. I still struggled with the amount of fuss required to look presentable, when I lived with my father, a simple tunic dress sufficed for any time of the day or night, even a sack-cloth was quite appropriate as my father really never noticed what I wore or how I looked. What I said, what I thought, these were the important qualities to him. Now the situation was quite reversed. When I tried to engage Sarah in the philosophy of ideas or tell her that *Lysistrata* was a brilliant work of satire, involving woman's issues, she would either yawn or pout telling me that she couldn't imagine reading anything other than her own social schedule; and so it was we found ourselves at the vicar's tea-dance on that memorable summer's day.

As Sarah weaved her way into the centre of the room, blonde ringlets gleaming, I found a settee placed beneath a picture window overlooking the garden. I sat down rather wistfully looking outside wondering how quickly I could escape. My thoughts turned to *The Odyssey* and the hero's struggles; how much easier it must be, I thought, to be a man, to have the independence to slay dragons and travel the world. I was learning that a woman's lot in civilized society involved much waiting and patience, at least here in Haddington.

With my thoughts far away, I didn't notice the presence of a young man in the room. Seeing me gazing wistfully out the window, he cleared his throat.

"Harrumph," he said. "I'm Thomas Chappard, just returned from India. It appears as though everyone else is in the other room. Who are you?"

I looked up, startled. "Oh, hello," I replied. "I'm Guinevere Jones. I'm staying over at Haddington Hall with my cousins."

"Really. How extraordinary. I've known that family all my life and never heard of you. Wherever did you come from?"

I looked at him sharply feeling a little vexed at his question. "I don't think that's any of your concern."

He had clearly touched a nerve with me. While I was happy to debate an intellectual idea, I found it exceedingly uncomfortable to discuss my background. When I was with my father, I knew my identity and place in the world, now, here in Haddington, I felt quite adrift.

"Oh, I'm terribly sorry," he said. I didn't mean to embarrass you. I tend to be somewhat outspoken which is a constant problem for me. I only received my commission with the army due to my father's record. Left to my own devices, I would be quite hopeless as I'm really rather socially inept. Look, would you like to go for a walk? I'm not much of a dancer, I'm afraid."

My face brightened at the prospect of going outside. "I'd like that very much. Really, I would. I can't dance at all."

He opened the French windows to the freedom of the garden. "Extraordinary. Oh, I've done it again. Look, I'm terribly sorry. I've never met a girl who didn't like to dance."

"Actually, I, for one, am pleased you say whatever's on your mind. That's terribly refreshing."

"Oh," he said, and smiled. "Well, Miss Jones, I think you and I are about to become very good friends."

As we talked and walked in the sun-drenched gardens, I finally felt at home again. I told him about my upbringing, my love for books and philosophy. He, in turn, told me that a military life was similar to boarding school: there were strict rules to follow, and yet, those who rose through the ranks were somehow those who could bend the rules in such a way there was an inherent advantage to their commanding officer. He explained that if it were as simple as everyone merely following the rules and adhering to guidelines, than any old plodder would rise to be Brigadier-General. But clearly that was not the case. He told me that a surprising number of good soldiers remained at the bottom of the heap, perhaps because they really were good soldiers.

"They lacked imagination," he said, "and were content to follow rules. But here's the paradox. One can't be seen to break the rules either as that would get you booted out."

I found I understood his theory and realized that I had, in this man, met someone surprisingly similar to my own father: they both understood their respective landscapes and could decipher and discern the code to achieve their ends. My father's inner world and Mr. Chappard's outer world shared a common understanding: imagination combined with discernment was key.

During the walk home, I listened to Sarah's chatter about the inept men she had met; no one it seemed could measure up to her ideal: he would be dashing and handsome, diplomatic and wealthy; all the other woman would want him, of course, and he would only have eyes for Sarah. Despite my own limited experience with men, I couldn't help but wonder if Sarah would ever be content. If her ideal man didn't exist in the village, could he be found at all?

Over the next week, I found myself guarding my meeting with Mr. Chappard, Thomas, Tom, as I liked to call him in my private inner realm, as though it were the most delicious secret that I couldn't quite bring myself to share with the rest of the world, small though that world may be. So it wasn't until the following weekend that I found myself surprised by the arrival of a beautifully engraved invitation, inviting me to luncheon at the old manor next door. As etiquette would have it, Sarah and her mother were also cordially invited to the event as the families had been neighbours for centuries.

To my surprise, Sarah was surprisingly reticent about this invitation, almost coy, saying only that she didn't know he had returned from service in India. Nevertheless, Sarah said inviting them for luncheon was the 'very least' they could do, considering the closeness of the families. As I pressed her for more information, Sarah only said there had been 'an understanding', which would be discussed at a later date.

Lunch was a small, elegant affair, with no more than twelve guests. I was seated across the table from Tom, and Sarah was placed at the other end near Mr. Whitterly, whom by all accounts, despite possessing a reasonable fortune, had suffered the indignity of a failed career. His work as a vicar was exceedingly short-lived. His sermons, it seemed, did not measure up to popular expectation, insufficient hell and brimstone, being the common verdict, as he tended to err on the meek and mild side of things. I could see that Sarah was not at all pleased at the attention he was giving her, wondering perhaps what people would think if he started courting her; though judging by his inability to eat more than a morsel of quail, she had quite captivated him without the least effort.

I turned my attention back to Mr. Chappard agreeing with his assessment that life really was wasted on those who had no interest in intellectual pursuits.

"How dull it would be," he said, "if we couldn't use our minds to expand beyond the life we currently inhabit."

"Is that what kept you going in India," I asked him? "During the months of routine engagement when you had nothing to do?"

"Of course," he replied. "From the army's perspective, there were always things to do, but these weren't always tasks that interested me."

"I know what you mean," I said. "Here in Haddington, I can't believe that women haven't been taught how to think, most can barely read. Their lives are practically confined within the four walls of their front room, with an occasional airing."

"You make it sound like the life of a horse," said Tom, smiling. "Surely the lives of the fairer sex are not as dull as you portray. What about those dances you so despise?"

"I guess," I replied, "If I did fit into civilized society and knew how to dance, I would be an entirely different type of woman, and not at all myself."

"You'd be right in that respect. You are a most unusual woman, and one whom I would like to know much better." He lowered his voice as he asked me to meet him outside after tea. "We will be breaking up into separate rooms shortly, the men in one and the ladies in the other. But after one or maybe two cups of tea, you will be able to make an excuse to break away, perhaps go for a walk. Meet me at the fountain near the Italian garden. I'll wait for you."

As expected, Sarah found time during the tea-break to tell me how miserable she was sitting next to Mr. W.

"Did you see how his cheeks became red? He is an over-stuffed bird of a man, twitter, twitter, twitter. I thought he would never stop plying me with questions and asking me what I like to do, all in the vain hope, no doubt, that I would somehow, someday condescend to go with him. Ha. Not a chance. And you, lucky thing, were seated across the table from the Colonel himself."

"Truly?" I said. "He didn't tell me he was a Colonel, only that he's on leave from India."

"Oh, yes," replied Sarah. "He really is the biggest catch. And one that I don't intend to let get away." With that, she turned her attention to a question from her mama.

I saw that as my queue to escape the dreadful menagerie of female company and quietly escape to the gardens. I didn't need my cloak as the weather held.

I saw him framed against the backdrop of the sundial, a tall, lean figure. He turned and held his arms out to me; I found myself wrapped in his embrace.

"Guinevere," he said. "This may be sudden, but I love you. I'm not doing anything by the book and this is improper, so please forgive me. I know I shouldn't be asking you directly without meeting your father, but...will you do me the honour of becoming my wife? It's sudden but I'm returning to India very soon, any day now, and I can't, won't, leave you behind...I couldn't bear to make that trip without you...would you possibly..."

"Oh," I said, my heart leaping. "Tom, may I call you Tom...yes, yes...yes," feeling so much that I wanted to tell him everything in my heart and not caring for the lack of propriety, never being one to stand on protocol anyway.

"I think I loved you from that first moment".

"I also believe in love at first sight," he said. "Have you read Plato?"

"Of course," I replied. "Are you referring to *The Republic*? And the idea of soul mates?"

"Yes, I don't think we can really love anyone we don't know from before..."

"I know. I agree. But I would like my father to attend the wedding."

"Of course you do. Send him a letter today and see if he can arrive within the fortnight. I'm sorry to rush things my darling but ...well, there's no point in waiting, is there? "

"We don't need permission from my Aunt, do we," I asked, suddenly worried. I am of age. And you are...?"

"Old enough to know exactly what I'm doing. Don't worry about a thing. It will all work out."

"Alright," I said, almost dancing on air. "But I really think I should tell my Aunt later today that I must contact my father in the most urgent way."

"Do what you must," he replied. "But as shocking as this will sound to Haddington, I intend to marry you with or without your father's approval. Does that sound terribly arrogant?"

"I wouldn't change a thing about you," I replied. "And I have a feeling my father would whole-heartedly approve of your resolve."

"I have a feeling we'll get along famously," he said. "We'd better go back inside before they send out a search party."

"Alright," I agreed. "But promise me we can make our news public within the week. I don't expect it will take more than three or four days to hear back from Cambridge once my father receives the news."

"Next weekend then? We'll plan an official engagement party for next Saturday. But we won't be able to see each other before then – we need to pay some attention to protocol. Agreed?"

"Yes, I can live with that. Oh, Tom, yes, I've thought of you as Tom, I have to call you Tom, why are you looking at me like that, not Thomas, since we've first met. You don't mind, do you?"

"Of course not," he responded. I've only thought of you as...Guinevere. Such a beautiful name. And I wouldn't dream of shortening it either...just so you know."

"My father was influenced by Mallory," I replied. "Lancelot, Guinevere, the Knights of the Round Table."

"From my perspective, the name Lancelot wouldn't have worked so well in the army," he said. "I'd have been a laughing stock, but you know I'll be true to you, don't you. You know I love you, there's no doubt. Always."

"Yes," I said, "always and forever."

The couple returned to the main house to find the party breaking up. Sarah looked thunderous to see her cousin arrive with the Colonel and told her rather sharply they needed to return home immediately.

The girls walked home in virtual silence; Sarah's mother had taken the carriage home earlier in the day, and hadn't given a reason for her early departure. I thought she suffered from heat stroke or headaches at the first sign of warmer weather but perhaps that was uncharitable; perhaps she simply wanted the young people to socialize on their own. It was hard to fathom these people and their world; sometimes it seemed societal rules prevailed and other times they didn't. But today, something felt different; Sarah was chilly, almost rude. It was as though we hadn't been living under the same roof for the past six months, almost as though we were total strangers and had just met. I hoped the news of my engagement to Tom could restore some good humor; perhaps I had overstayed my welcome.

Our return to Haddington Hall was met with news of an early dinner. I didn't quite know how to broach the topic of my engagement given the general tone of things at the moment; I didn't want to pretend I hadn't spent time with the Colonel as Sarah called him, but I hoped to ease my way into the topic without seeming to step on any toes. As fate would have it, the conversation came to me before I could reach for it.

"Guinevere, Sarah informs me that you spent time alone with Colonel Chappard this afternoon. You need to know there has been an understanding of betrothal between the two families for as long as I can remember. Thomas invited Sarah to this summer luncheon to encourage connection between the two families, and you, my dear, must remember that as chaperone to Sarah, you are merely an afterthought, invited out of politeness; it is really most inappropriate to leave Sarah's side, especially to spend time alone with a young man. Do I make myself clear?"

I felt at a complete lost. I couldn't tell them Tom had asked me to marry him without making a total fool of myself. I trusted him completely. Absolutely I did. And yet, why did he not tell me there was an understanding between him and Sarah? This made no sense at all. I hadn't seen them together, not once, and what I knew of Tom, Sarah's idle prattle would bore him more quickly than ...well, practically anything I could think of. I simply didn't see them together. And yet, I really wasn't in a position to share my secret with them. I could only mutely nod in response to the question asked of me, yes, I understood that my involvement with Tom was not, would not be welcomed by this family, which placed me in a very awkward position. All I could do was write my father urgently and inform him of my engagement. I wouldn't, and couldn't, expect help from my Aunt, nor did I want to give up this man. What a terrible mess I was in. Then there was the engagement party next Saturday. What is the etiquette around that, I wondered? Could I keep this engagement a secret in a village like Haddington? Not likely, I surmised. Perhaps tomorrow would bring an answer: A new day, a new beginning. I pleaded a headache and asked to be excused from the table. Sarah smirked, feeling no doubt that her mother's ammunition had found a likely target, whereas my Aunt merely nodded her regal head dismissing me to my own devices.

I wrote a letter to my father that night asking him to respond on an urgent basis. Ideally, if at all possible, I needed him to make the trip next weekend. Although that wouldn't give him long to prepare for the journey, I hoped he could make it down in time for Saturday evening where he could, at the very least, meet Tom. There was an urgency attached to this arrangement as Tom thought he could be shipped out in a fortnight – and he wanted me to go with him. Life moves very quickly at times, I wrote, but I knew how to make good use of this once-in-a-lifetime opportunity. This stroke of good fortune was what I knew he wanted for me, perhaps even had in mind for me when he sent me to Haddington Hall. I was so blessed, I wrote, to have Tom in my life.

Four days later, my letter, unopened, was returned to me. Addressee unknown. But how could that be? I had written him only last month; things were fine, he was preparing his students for their latest set of exams. It seemed like a good move and he was in fine spirits. And now? I realized I had no choice at this point. I was truly at the mercy of my Aunt. I needed to confide in her, whatever the cost to myself; I realized that she may have already received an invitation for Saturday evening, in which case, she would not be the most willing ally. I tried to prepare myself for this discussion, mentally rehearsing in my mind the whirlwind relationship with Tom. I knew how to debate, I reasoned, I could construct a sound argument as well as anyone, so somehow, someway, I needed to reach her, have her hear me out without fear of recrimination. I had, after all, done nothing wrong. I had followed my heart, and my heart led me to Tom.

I entered the green room where my Aunt normally took her morning tea. As anticipated, she was by herself, Sarah has wondered off to review one of her outfits, no doubt, and left her mama to enjoy some rare solitude.

"Aunt," I replied. "I must talk to you about my father."

"Oh?" she said, eyebrow arching, "what in the world has he done now? That man has no sense of propriety whatsoever."

"The thing is," I said, "I wrote to him earlier this week on a rather urgent matter, and his letter has been returned to me unopened. Have you heard from him?"

"Dear child, I would be the last person in whom your father would confide, although if you can't reach him at the College, I suspect he has drank himself into a stupor. It wouldn't be the first time."

"I don't believe you," I said. "He's not like that."

"Why do you think he didn't teach in a College before this time? They wouldn't have him. Now, why are you attempting to contact him anyway? I thought you were settling in to your life here at Haddington Hall."

"Yes, Aunt, I am, but," I hesitated for a moment, "I don't want you to be cross with me but Tom, the

Colonel, has asked me to marry him. Return to India with him."

"I wondered when you would come out with that. Sarah told me you were cooking something up, you ungrateful girl, even though I told you he is not yours for the taking. I won't hear of it, do you hear me? I simply will not allow you to steal what does not belong to you. First of all there was your mother, yes; I dare speak of her to you, as no one else will. Mad as a hatter. She was sent to a nunnery in France. Better off in an insane asylum, I said. She had no right bearing a child, especially in her state; and leaving my brother to care for you. "

"Ungodly is what it was. And now, I take charity on you, bring you into my home, care for you as my own daughter and this is how you repay me. I won't have it, do you hear me? I won't have it."

I felt more bewildered than angry. What did she expect me to do? To say? I didn't ask to come here any more than I planned to fall in love with the Colonel. My Aunt made it sound as though it were some sort of nefarious plot I had concocted with my poor mother, may she rest in peace, wherever she was, to upset their carefully ordered lives. It wasn't that way at all. Life just happens. I knew that. My father knew that. Well, he had taught me that life happens and I was sure he knew enough to guide me in that area. The drinking himself into a stupor didn't make any sense to me. I never saw him drink. Not at all.

"Just the other week, I heard news from Cambridge that he suffered some sort of fit, presumably brought on by too much alcohol. I wanted to spare you the news, but now that you insist on bringing this all up..."

"And you weren't going to tell me? How long were you going to keep this from me?"

"Oh, for heaven's sake, no need for the theatrics. Dry your eyes. I'll send you in a carriage tomorrow and you can find out what you can. The college bursar may know where he is. I don't."

"But, it's Thursday already. I'm due to have my dinner engagement with Tom on Saturday night; we planned it last week."

"That's already taken care of; it's quite impossible. I received an invitation as you might expect the day before yesterday and replied that you would be out of town until the following week. I understand he will not be shipping out to India quite as quickly as he anticipated. His commanding officer is, or was, rather good friends with my late husband; the Colonel's posting back to India is indefinitely delayed meaning there is no urgency whatsoever."

"But..." I stumbled on my words, becoming increasingly aware of the gravity of the situation. Tom did not expect me this weekend, furthermore, he was told I was out of town; I was a virtual prisoner in this house, and had no way of getting word to him. Perhaps I could sneak out after dinner, run through the village, and see him? Oh, what did I care what people thought? What did I care? This wasn't how I was raised. I only knew that my heroes and heroines would fight any battle to be with the one they loved; truth would out, wouldn't it?

"Under the circumstances, I suggest you pack immediately and take the carriage to Cambridge this afternoon. There is no point in waiting until the morning. You should set your mind at rest today. "

I wondered if my Aunt could sense my anxiety at leaving Tom and simply wanted to prevent me wandering through the village in the middle of the night. If she had already told him that I was out of town, it would be nearly impossible to try and see him in the next day or two; far better to wait until I found out what really happened to my father and then return to Haddington. It appeared as though I didn't have any choice in the matter.

I set to work writing Tom a note that he would receive in the afternoon's post. At the very least, the mail was efficient and I knew it would reach him. I told him that my father had disappeared and I needed to leave town that day. I was sorry that I would not have the chance to see him in person but under the circumstances, given my Aunt's animosity towards the union, I felt that I should see my father as soon as possible. I hoped Tom would understand that I didn't want to delay the wedding, but without my father's support, I was in a very difficult situation. I hoped he would understand.

I placed my few possessions, books and clothing in a small portable case, thinking that these last six months had changed me more than I realized. By meeting Tom, I had achieved the heart of a woman; I knew that I was loved; knew that I was safe.

I looked for Sarah, wishing to say good-bye to her but she was nowhere to be found. I didn't have time to look further afield than the music room and the conservatory so asked my Aunt to say good-bye on my behalf.

I climbed into the carriage hoping to be in Cambridge by nightfall. I was hopeful that a room would be made available to me as a courtesy, and in any case, my father had left me a small amount of money that could be used in an emergency; although it wasn't enough to give me any sort of livelihood, I could certainly find my way back to Haddington and Tom.

The first part of the journey passed quickly. I found myself lost in thought and didn't notice the route: was it scenic or uninspiring? I had no idea. We reached Cambridge within three hours and I found my way to the office of the registrar. When I explained who I was, and understood my father had disappeared or even died, the bursar simply shook his head and said he didn't think so.

"More likely left for France. An urgent message arrived from his wife; she had taken ill," he said, "and he needed to take a sabbatical. Apart from that, there was no problem. Your father is, or was, very much alive last week. His mail wasn't being forwarded, which is why it was returned to sender."

He then gave me the address of a convent near Lyon, in France.

I had sufficient funds to cross the English Channel. Although I had never been outside England, I needed to get to the bottom of this peculiar situation and address the issue of my parents, if only for Tom's sake. Again I wrote Tom telling him of my latest plan, explaining that I fully hoped to be back in England within the month. As my father, it now seemed, was not missing, I would be able to invite him to the wedding after all. Be of good faith, I added, I will see you soon.

I arrived in Lyon and secured accommodation for the night. It would be an easy trip to the Convent, which was located only a few miles away.

When I reached St. Mary's the next morning, I was greeted by the Mother Superior. She told me that I looked a lot like my mother but I had arrived too late to meet this woman whom I would never know. She had taken ill and succumbed to the recent influenza that was sweeping England and

France; only 48 hours ago they had laid her to rest, poor soul, but my father had made it there on time to say his last good-byes.

I hardly knew what to say; I wouldn't now have the chance to meet this woman who had given me life but had not been part of my life. Now she was gone. I felt a pang of loss for all I had never known. Was she really as mad as my Aunt had suggested? Or was that just another story as well? I needed to find my father; he must be nearby. I asked the Holy Mother if my father would see me.

"Oh, yes," replied Mother Superior, "He is staying at lodgings not far from here. He'll probably return to England today but you should still reach him if you hurry. It will take you about a half an hour to walk there – follow the road 'round the other side of the hill and you'll come to a farmer's cottage. He took a room there for the week."

I set off to find my father – so much to tell him. I was determined to get to the bottom of this mystery as well. Why did he suddenly come to France when he hadn't been in contact with my mother all these years?

I knocked on the door of a small farmhouse – the only one in the area so I assumed I had found the right place. A red-cheeked, plump woman answered the door. "Oui?" she said. I suddenly realized that my French was not as proficient as it should be – I hoped I could make myself understood.

I have come to visit my father, I stuttered in halting French. I was told by the Mother Superior that he was staying with you.

"La bas," she said, pointing to the barn and shut the door in my face. I shrugged my shoulders. They were French after all. Perhaps not as polite as the English?

I made my way across the field to the oversized barn. I called out to my father hoping that I would find him. "Father? It's Guinevere. Are you there?"

"Guinevere?" I heard a rasping voice answer me in response. "Don't come in, I have influenza. It's contagious."

"Oh, I'm not bothered with that," I said bravely. "I've come all this way. Whatever is going on? What are you doing in France?"

"How did you find me?" he said in response. I thought you were safely tucked away in Haddington."

"I was," I replied, peering around the corner to see an area in the corner with a cot laid in between the rough flooring. "I'm engaged to a wonderful man called Tom, I wanted to ask you for your blessing and invite you to the wedding, so I...." Her father's face was pasty and he looked as though he hadn't eaten for a month. "Father...!"

"It's alright, I'm dying. I know. I wanted to spare you."

"But what happened? Why didn't you contact me?"

"I thought I would make a quick trip over to France to see your mother. I know, I never mentioned her, but she became very ill after your birth, wasn't in her right mind at the time, so I brought her to this convent in France. She slowly became better but became used to the way of life over here. We thought it easier if you didn't know her. The quiet, contemplative life suited her."

"Auntie said she was mad as a hatter."

"That's not the entire truth. She recovered herself in later years and we've kept in touch. She contacted me only weeks ago, on her death bed – tuberculosis they call it. Looks like I've got it now."

I tried to come closer to him wanting to offer him comfort. "No child. I don't want to pass this on to you as well."

"But..."

"There is nothing you can do for me, I only have a day or two left. I've left instructions at the College. My last will and testament. Dear child, we've had a good life together. Don't cry for me."

"I know. I just...there's so much I want to share with you. My engagement, Tom; oh, father, you would so like him."

"I'm happy for you. I knew you would have the opportunities you needed once you went out into society. And are you being treated well?"

"Yes, like a member of the family."

"Then I have nothing to worry about." He started coughing again. "Give me that water there will you? Yes, that's it. I really can't have you risk getting sick here. Go back to England today, if you can. That's a good girl. Good-bye."

I turned away not knowing what to do. I had come all this way only to discover my mother dead and my father dying. I couldn't leave him alone. I decided to find a room at the Convent. As they had known my mother all these years, surely they couldn't begrudge a bit of space to her only daughter?

I managed to secure a room and stayed on to nurse my father over the next few weeks. He had such little strength, it was all I could do let him know that I was not going back to England. Several weeks later, he died.

By this time, I had written again to Tom but hadn't heard back from him. I only had the mailing address of the Covent, but I was surprised he didn't send me word.

A few days after my father's death, I did hear from Sarah. She said with great bitterness that despite her mother's efforts, Tom had returned to India. It seemed entirely evident, she said, that I would not be returning any time soon and Tom believed that I had left him. He had been told that madness ran in my family and, as I had, on a whim, left the country, too afraid perhaps to enter into the state of holy matrimony, he had no choice but return to India without me.

As I had not heard from Tom, it did seem likely that he had gone abroad without me.

I wondered if he had received any of my letters? Surely he would have known I was speaking the truth; but if my letters were intercepted, if he didn't read them, perhaps he really did think I was mad.

Now there was nothing left for me in England. I couldn't return to Haddington Hall, and I had no father. All I could do was stay on in France at the Convent. I didn't live long. Six months later, I also succumbed to the TB epidemic. Despite my great expectations, there was nothing more for me. I died with a broken heart thinking of the great love that might have been.

Although Guinevere wasn't able to be with the man she loved, there is an increasing sense of integration in this life. The qualities of the 4th chakra representing the heart centre were well-

balanced and there appeared to be a feeling of hope. Guinevere loved her father and later fell deeply in love with Tom.

However, there was also a wound, which ran like a river through this incarnation. She didn't have a mother and felt that loss more deeply than she realized. Guinevere was able to access her feelings and take actions, but lacked the feminine influence.

In my current lifetime, I was able to begin a romantic relationship in my 20s, and make big decisions such as moving countries or changing jobs. But I suffered in childhood from serious pneumonia and bronchial infections. Similar to Guinevere, I didn't have early bonding with a mother. I didn't know how to be present to the receptive feminine energy, and needed to better balance the yin and the yang.

Perhaps creative self-expression in the 5th chakra will show me the way?

Chapter Five

5th Chakra - Colour Blue

The throat chakra is all about self-expression, communication and growth.

Balanced: Loyal, trustworthy, tactful, calm.

Out-of-balance: Unfaithful, untrustworthy, cold, self-righteous.

The Unfaithful Doctor

It wasn't until 2005 that I saw HIM again – my husband in a former life. It proved to be a source of embarrassment as I found myself sexually attracted, very sexually attracted, to this tall, lean man who could have been, and most probably was, twenty or thirty years older than myself. He seemed to have a Svengali, almost hypnotic, influence on me and I couldn't quite leave him alone. But that's all I can say. I can't really tell you what he looked like for if I did, friends of mine, still alive, would recognize the description and tell him that I included him in my book. Would he be flattered or outraged? The former I think. I suspect he secretly likes the fact that it took me time to get over him; (mind you a century and a half is pushing the envelope): but in any case, the whole business reminded me of Carlie Simon's song: "He's so vain, you probably think this song…is about you, don't you…" even 150 years after the fact. But he'll never know the whole truth;

not least, because the truth is so truly bizarre that he wouldn't believe me even if I sat down and told him, which I won't. Obviously.

When we met, (I can't tell you when or where for reasons of confidentiality), I was only 30-something; even then, he, (I'll just call him 'H' for HIM), reminded me of Prince Philip in his older years, which gave me to believe he was at least 63 – H – not Prince P. (The latter, of course, is absolutely ageless.) I may be giving HIM the benefit of the doubt – perhaps he was closer to 70 by that time – which is why I fully admit to being an ageist when it comes to men. And why not? Men routinely pick up, or marry, women who are several decades younger than the original model. From this perspective, I feel entitled to discount the attentions of a man so much older than myself, especially a man whom, by all accounts, was entirely penniless. (And even if I didn't discount the attention of this man, who was way too old, (and penniless), you would have thought he would at least have remembered me. I mean, how could he have forgotten me?

I felt entitled, no, I wanted to discount my feelings for a man so much older than myself, who couldn't give me what I wanted in (my current) life, namely marriage, love and a financially secure future together. He had been married, (in this life), umpteen times, 4, 5 or 6 at least); I lost count after 1973, (at which point he had either become a nudist or had twins), can't remember now as I was so fixated on the numbers, (meaning his advanced age), floating around in my head. By the time he had exchanged the most unholiest of vows with the third or fourth Mrs. H. I was barely toddling in my diapers. It was extraordinary. What did I see in this man? I was also extremely puzzled why he was throwing, and I do mean projectile vomiting, sexual energy my way so that even I couldn't miss it, and then when I gave him an opportunity to follow through, he claimed he was only looking for friendship. What a tease!

Perhaps this accounts for my hostility towards this man. He was a flirt, and a tease. This much married-man engaged my affections under false pretenses. Friends don't flirt. Do they? Friends don't hold hands and caress, do they? Unless they are friends 'with benefits' and as far as I remembered, he wasn't paying into the plan...so, our relationship was more like strangers who knew each other, sort of, and I still wasn't sure about the friend part.

It wasn't fair. No, more than that. It was just plain wrong. He didn't know I recognized him from a past-life, (and I do mean a literal past-life), which can be one of the pitfalls of being psychic. Even though a century or two may have passed, if you are born 'open' like me, when you see these men again, it's no different than running into an ex you didn't want to see at that cocktail party last month. And I really didn't want to see him again, especially as he was bound and determined to treat me no differently than during our last go-round. How's that for bad karma? Even if you don't get it 'right' in one life, they pop up, just like that, right in front of you.

In this case, I had no choice but to relive the past. God help me, was that a wise choice? What if I got stuck and couldn't get back. But no, I assured myself, I knew what I was doing. I wouldn't completely lose control – or track – of my current consciousness. I could review the past-life in a semi-dream state or dive right in, similar to a deep hypnotic trance. I hoped this would give me the answers to the rather uncomfortable questions that were plaguing my current life. I took a deep breath and searched my consciousness for the information…where would I find myself, and who would I be?

I found myself in rural Virginia in the year 1835. I was a fine-boned, rather slight woman with dark hair and eyes, descended from the Metis people. I was born in French speaking Canada but somehow ended up across the border married to an American surgeon. Ah, yes, there he was. Such a handsome man: tall, blue eyes, nicely put together as though every bone and sinew was designed by a master craftsman, nothing wasted. When we met, I felt as though he was on a mission from the Great Creator as he helped the wounded and the dying, risking his own life to tend the sick. It wasn't long before he realized that my father was the medicine man for our people, a powerful shaman in his own right who also understood the sick – the sick of soul - were the people mostly tended by my father; some were possessed by evil spirits; others were simply sick at heart and felt dispossessed after fighting on the side of the British in 1812.

It was a bad time for us all; we lost so many; regardless of our petty squabbles, we hadn't imagined so many of our people could die so quickly. Although Upper Canada didn't fall to the Americans, there was still much loss of life and Tecumseh was now dead. I was not descended from his people, I was a half-breed, a Metis, but my father taught me about the old ways. He hadn't expected to enter into union with a white woman, (for at the time of their ceremonial marriage, he was a full-blood Lakota and anyone with mixed blood was considered more white than aboriginal). But my mother, similar to myself, was also darker skinned with a slight build. She said her colouring was due to Cree in her bloodline and the women in her family were all small of stature with dark hair.

I often wondered what would have happened if one of my ancestors had married a fair-haired man with blue eyes, but mother said this had never happened, not that it couldn't happen mind you, as there was no reason why a white-haired, blue eyed man wouldn't move to our small community near Trois-Rivieres, but it simply hadn't happened yet.

Perhaps, she said to me, some day I would be the one to change all this: perhaps, I would be given the gift of second sight as my father was a shaman, she said that it would be entirely possible that I would be the one to receive this gift; I had argued at the time that surely this would be

inherited through the male line, if I had any brothers, (which I didn't), it made sense to me that he, or they, would have inherited the shamanic gifts of my father, including the ability to see into the other worlds and beyond. But, no, insisted my mother, my father worked in the underworld, not the upperworld, and with this explanation she changed the subject once again. I had always detected a reluctance to pursue this line of questioning with her. On the one hand, she told me always that being of mixed-blood was a great gift for we more than other peoples, could move between the worlds; we spoke several languages, and she said that language was everything. But even then, I wondered, what did language give her? Did she really live the life she wanted? She didn't have the education or background. And she would never fit into the 'establishment'. She helped raise her sisters but didn't know how to read. She had a knack for brewing home-made potions and remedies; I always thought this is why she ended up with my father, they complemented each other: he worked his magic within the soul, and despite her lack of formal training, more often than not, her ability to brew or mix the right herb at the right time did seem to save lives and especially stem poisoning in the blood. More than anything, she became known for her ability to cure people with serious blood problems. Why this was so, I really couldn't say, but her ability allowed our family to live well; we even received gifts from people who had given up hope of finding a cure.

I do know I was destined to meet Dr. Henry Longfield. He appeared with the other civilians and soldiers during that horrible period after York had been attacked. Many people were afraid that Montreal would fall and there was talk of bolstering our defenses in all our towns and villages. We couldn't lose our language and our home. We couldn't, wouldn't, be annexed and forced to join the states to our south. We were a British Colony; they weren't. The border was there for a reason. At least that's what people thought and I had no reason to disagree.

Before I met Henry, I don't recall meeting an American person. I suspected there weren't so different to us; they didn't speak as many languages, of course, only their own brand of the English language, which I guessed they called American. Surely they wouldn't consider the language they spoke English since they were so determined to achieve separation from the mother country?

He came to our community, he said, in case we were engulfed in war. He said there were plenty of doctors across the way in Michigan, and more doctors than patients near Niagara Falls, but here, he wondered if we even had any doctors. I looked at my mother. I guessed that she and my father were the closest thing we had to 'doctors' in our village, and I really didn't know what to say. Fortunately, she did. I never did see her at a loss for words – in any language.

"Dr. Longfield," she began.

"Oh, do call me Hal," he said.

"Certainly. We are a small village with perhaps one hundred and fifty people who call this home. Many of our men who could bear arms have gone to fight the cause, some, as you know, have come home and we hope, very much hope, the danger has passed. But, it is I, if anyone, who cares for the people here. I am not a doctor or a nurse. But I am skilled in the ways of the plants and it is the plants that heal our people."

"I see," he said, and looked my way. "And your daughter? Does she help you with these plants?"

"Cele is only 15 and has much to learn in the ways of the world. She has followed in the tradition of her father and dreams the future for us."

At this he smiled and looked off to one side as though conferring with an invisible friend. "I have heard of those who see the future but I didn't think you had witches here in Upper Canada."

"Not witches," said my mother firmly. "Come, I will show you." She marched ahead of us through the front door into the vast expanse of land behind our cabin. "If you look up into the sky, you will see symbols; if you look into the earth, you will hear what you need to know. Our people are one with the land and the land talks to us. Cele is very good at listening. That is all. A witch is a magical creature created largely by men who are afraid of female power. But they also understand the laws of nature. A woman true to herself understands instinctively all there is to know – especially about men. This freedom of self-expression had frightened men - especially those who seek to control. That is the truth of witches here in our part of the world. Cele – go now – and see to our evening meal. I am sure the doctor has traveled a long way and needs food."

As I walked away to prepare a simple meal, I felt as though I was floating; a giddy feeling of delight came over me such as I had never experienced before. Those dark blue eyes, the colour of a winter storm, had blazed with an intensity and projected an energy towards me as we stood and chatted in the far corner of the field. Did that mean...? Could that mean he liked me? I wondered. Perhaps tonight would be the time to use those powers of which my mother had spoken: perhaps I could look into my own future and see what fate held in storage for me?

We were interrupted at dinner by the return of my father, the shaman. He took one look at the doctor and said they must speak urgently, in private. Dr. Longfield agreed and followed my father outside. My sisters continued to chat as though nothing unusual had happened, but I suspected something monumental, something, I didn't know what, that would change the course of our entire lives was occurring at the back door.

I never knew what was said between them; I only heard the sounds of hooves galloping away. Some time later, Dr. Longfield returned, accompanied by a Jesuit priest. It seemed that Dr. Longfield was about to be married – to me.

Years later when I looked back on that evening, I should have realized it all happened too quickly but at the time, I was very young and a little in love.

We returned to his native Virginia where I was considered something of an oddity. As a young woman, I was considered sturdy enough to risk child-birth and young brides were by no means unusual. My skin colour, a little darker than normal, was considered different, but I'd have to say it was more my own attitude that created the separation with the other young wives: they seemed to need each other, whereas I needed no one, not even my husband.   I discovered there was a subtle difference between wanting and needing. As the years went by, I did everything to please my husband: gave him children and kept everyone healthy by passing on the skills I learned from my own mother.   But my husband grew increasingly distant. When he discovered that my ability to dream the future did not include giving him practical day-to-day advice on events and outcomes, he lost interest in me. Much of his time was spent gambling and chasing women, always under the guise of being a caring doctor.

I eventually died at the age of 45 from nothing more dramatic than loneliness.

As I came out of this self-induced trance and looked at the events in this life, I see the vulnerability I experienced as this young girl Cele. In a way, her family had sold her to this man; they knew nothing about him, and yet allowed their daughter who, by all accounts, did have some unusual gifts, to marry him. But I suppose that was the way of the world: even in small communities, too many mouths to feed were a liability. And yet, Cele had felt he was her destiny – he didn't treat her well, almost held her in contempt. I wondered what it was about this man that allowed her to recognize him as her mate despite the rather sad outcome. If nothing else, this past-life helped explain the link between 'H" and Henry. I suppose I was more fortunate this time around: I didn't fall into his magnetic trap.

(There was a reason why at an earlier age in my life, I would repeat the phrase like a mantra: "God save me from charming Englishmen", due in no small part to the not inconsiderable charm displayed by my first great love who happened to be English.)

Although I was magnetically attracted to 'H', those characteristics I grew to despise in that life: his flirtatious behaviour and inability to handle money, were repeated in this life.

I came to realize that unless there is a true desire for change within a soul, we do come back again and again with similar characteristics and qualities. Perhaps that is the true meaning of suffering: repeating the same behaviour lifetime after lifetime, without a new beginning.

For me, this is the benefit of accessing the soul's wisdom: once we learn the lesson, we really can climb off that wheel of karma, rather than literally marrying the same person over and over with the only difference being a new time period, and different body.

As the throat chakra is about self-expression, communication and growth, I achieved mixed reviews in that life. Although I was loyal, trustworthy, tactful and calm, my husband was unfaithful, untrustworthy, cold, and self-righteous. He was always looking out for his own needs and interests; he put himself first and yet I felt helpless to make any change or speak out. Part of this was due to being a foreigner in a new country and feeling different to the others. The other part was my role as a woman.

I wondered how a woman could stand in her power without being judged, abandoned or ignored? Clearly there were more lessons for me to learn about balancing power and wisdom. I would begin to understand this lesson in my life as a temple priestess.

Chapter Six

6th Chakra - Colour Indigo

Brow chakra, associated with psychic ability and the qualities of time and light.   This chakra is impacted by the hypothalamus and is often called the third eye, which sees clairvoyantly or beyond the physical.

Balanced: Highly intuitive, clear-sighted, integrity, true, orderly mind.

Out-of-balance: Inability to trust intuition, scattered mind, inconsiderate, blinkered vision.

The Tale of the Priestess

I serve the temple priestess, linked to the cult of Isis, but our lineage is older, much older even than the great goddess herself. Some say we go back to the beginning of time; our purpose is to anchor consciousness on the planet, to be the dark in the light and the light in the dark, for consciousness is the Universal paradox: that which is unseen, and yet brings forth every thing into being.

That is the role of women, of the divine feminine, and yet much has been forgotten.

Women have forgotten their true power and strength in their quest to be like men. This is why this tale, my story, must be told: I, more than any one else, embodied consciousness. I was born and trained in this truth, and yet even I forgot. If I forgot, what hope is there for the world?

I remember the two Universal principles: the yin and the yang, dark and light; form and formless. One cannot exist without the other. And so it is with the masculine and feminine principle, the polarity of form and formless creates worlds upon worlds...and yet, how could I know, even with my knowing, despite the preparation and even the precautions, I would, at the end of the day, be as open and vulnerable as any other woman, for more than anything else, I came to realize that first and foremost, even more than existing as Divine Consciousness, I am woman. And as woman, I am human, as woman, I am vulnerable.

I am kept apart, isolated; separated like a human membrane or hymen from the outside world.

I am 13 years old. It is the day I began my menses or journey into womanhood. It is a sacred day of initiation by women, for women. There is blood flowing down my thigh, sweet and sticky. My stomach hurts. If I were to lie with a man they told me, I would produce a child. My time of fertility is now. But that is not my path.

At the age of 13, I know that I am different to the others. I see things the others don't see; I know things the others don't know and won't know.

I am what they call a seer or see-er. I was born with this gift and it is has stayed with me. Often times, people, mostly women, are born with knowing and then forget. When they forget what they know, this knowledge goes underground, into the deep cave within and sits in the bottom of the stomach waiting to be remembered, waiting to be re-awakened. But I know. And I remember. I know that I was brought into the high temple as a baby. I know it was an honour. I know it was part of the Divine Oneness. And I know that I will not complete the life I was destined to live. I know this fate lies before me: I know the what, but I don't know the why.

But today, my initiation into womanhood, becomes a new birth day for me; I leave my facsimile of childhood to experience the delights of my new womanly body; the other women join me in this initiation as is our way; they drink deeply of my blood for we are sisters bonded in our female bodies. I accept and I submit.

The way of The Order is larger than my own identity for if I exist at all, the little 'I', with a will of its own, is only to be of service to the Way, to convey that which I am shown. And so I become a vessel, a channel, a part of the Tao. I don't have choice: that which later became known as 'free-will' was binded at birth; I know no difference. Now, I will be cloistered from the outer world even more than before, but truly it is no sacrifice for how can I surrender that which I never had?

A receptacle for love. I am born into this lifetime to be a receptacle for love. Receptive. Receiving. Re-ceive. Re-turn. Re-born. Receive. Accept.

These are the words which become the mantra for my day, and for my life. As a receptacle for love I receive the adoration, the projection and the messiness of the many. They see me as an oracle and a saviour. I know that I do not save; merely illuminate.

Consciousness exists to reveal, wisdom exists to restore.

I often speak in cryptic chants so that those who have eyes to see, and ears to hear, will know the truth; but truth itself is often sheltered from the seeker like a proverbial harbour in a storm: when needed, it is no where to be found, when not required, it is impossible to miss.

Why is that? Why do you think?

You think because you do not know, and if you know, truth is obsolete, for in all the places in heaven and earth, no such animal exists as absolute truth, for truth in all its multi-faceted hues is constructed through the human personality. Hence, this person or that person says: *that is the truth, my truth, that is what I believe*; and yet, this truth walks a narrow line moving through a tiny door. In answer to a simple question: "Did you make love to my sister's husband?" The truth may well be 'yes' but in a larger perspective, was that your own husband in another time and place, therefore you only made love to your own husband, rather than your sister's husband? Such is the nature of the multi-dimensional soul.

So what level of 'reality' is your truth? And what is your reality? The only truth that counts is the truth within your soul. You know what really happened in that moment, in that instant, which could be perceived differently by another person. This is why we say that truth is sheltered from the seeker without the gift of illumination.

I help people see. Yes, I can see for them, review the path they have chosen and assess whether or not it is for their highest good. That is perhaps the best-known description of a seer; and yet...the more beneficial approach is to help people help themselves, for as they learn to see what lies within their very hearts, their eyes are opened. Seeing with the eyes is but observing the world; seeing with the heart takes greater skill and courage; courage therefore is found within the heart, and clarity is seeing beyond the physical eyes.

This is part of the teachings I have come to re-store or re-plenish. Even this simple philosophy has become little known; or perhaps the masses do not care, but it wasn't always this way. In my time, the highest accolade was the wisdom and clear-sightedness to accept the teachings of the heart, for this organ served as a navigational compass which enabled the human to rise in frequency. As the frequency increases, more spiritual gifts and more knowing unfolds, but as with all spiritual gifts, the end should not be sought for itself; don't seek to purify in order to receive spiritual gifts, seek purification because it is your destiny.

And purification was, is, my destiny. But at the time of this life, even with my rigorous training, I hadn't yet become master of my heart. Even though I knew I was a vessel, a vehicle for divine love to flow in me and through me, even though I only knew the Way of the Order, my heart in its innocence and purity, revealed an even deeper truth: that of the woman within.

Every morning at dawn, I walked to the River. I would often collect water and bring it back to my Sisters; I didn't need to perform this simple task but I enjoyed the feeling of being in my body, the simple physicality of the hard, dry earth beneath my feet and the cool, clear water sliding with one mind into the urn, giving me a sense of oneness with my environment.

For much of the day, my body was forced to be still as I sat in trance; although I continued to breathe in this state of altered-consciousness, my organs moved into deep relaxation, which meant I didn't have to worry about hunger or thirst; I still had the breath of life coursing through me, but it was as though my body breathed me and my identity, my little 'I', was subsumed into the Oneness of all creation as I became the vessel for the other-world.

Today, however, I felt more alive than ever before, more connected to the soft pink and golden rays of the early morning as though my heart had flown out of my body and in that moment become the sky, merging with the far horizon; I felt transcendent and free, aware of my physicality, and yet unbound by it. And even as I reveled in this ecstatic interplay of consciousness, despite my heightened senses, I felt a shadow come over me, bringing me back to the present: I was not alone. I turned.

On the far corner of the bank sat a half-clad man sitting in a meditative pose. He was facing east, seemingly unaware of my presence. What was he doing in this sacred place? Everyone knew that men were forbidden in the valley; it had been this way for centuries; in order to maintain the purity of the Order, (and remove temptation), men were not permitted within 200 miles of this sacred site. It was written. It was law. And yet here he was.

I found myself moving closer to the man as though drawn by an irresistible force – curiousity - perhaps or a force of nature? I didn't know. I wondered what language he spoke; perhaps he didn't know where he was; perhaps he was a lost soul. As I moved closer to him, I realized that my earlier transcendent moment meant that I had lost all claim to modesty and I was now completely naked, carrying only the water jug on my head.

He opened his eyes and looked into me as though in that moment we had known each other forever; and perhaps we had, we did: there was no separation, no barrier. The merging I felt in that moment was not unlike my glorious expression to the risen sun only moments before. I suddenly knew why men were forbidden in the Order and my heart understood what it meant to be a woman. The sexual chemistry between us was palpable even though I didn't know the nature of chemical relations between a man and a woman, I knew the feeling of kundalini rising through my base chakra up into my sacral; and this was even more intense. Standing in front of him, trembling, mesmerized, I couldn't look anywhere else other than in his eyes, seeing myself reflected back through his dark gaze. His eyes seemed to embody the depth of feeling and reflection that I could only imagine, and not imagine, for I had no experience with men. And yet my heart with all its training, my mind with all its knowing, wanted to physically merge and become one with him and I knew that would mean death. I would be defiled in the eyes of the Order, unable to perform my duties, no longer able to see. As this realization hit me, I began to back away, still, the man had not moved, nor had he spoken. Everything that existed between us was unsaid, part of the infinite and the formless. I ran. I didn't look back.

As I returned to the temple, I forced myself to move into empty mind: pure and translucent, remembering who and what I am, acknowledging my physical body garbed as a woman, but playing out the role of the infinite. If my sisters thought that anything unusual had happened, they didn't speak of it. And neither did I.

In this life I had an inner awareness of the balance between power and wisdom. I knew I was different and accepted that difference. Temptation was thrust in front of me in the form of the beautiful man and yes, I stumbled, but did not fall.

Some may say my choice was a result of training formed by habit rather than free will. But I feel the awareness in that life that I served a larger purpose is a significant spiritual principle. Spirituality can call for sacrifice but this sacrifice must be given freely to be considered a pure service.

Some years ago, I was given information about a spiritual path that my guides called The Pure Way. This discipline is beyond dogma, religion, country or creed. It is the way of the deep heart where the purpose of life becomes the Path of Love. Not physical love, not romantic love but Universal Love. This is perhaps the most difficult path to walk for the human self says: What about me? What about my, smaller 'I' personality feelings? Don't I count? And the answer is "yes". Every person counts, every personality counts, and every feeling counts and yet, there is a spiritual maturity that I grew into in that life epitomized by the third eye: awareness, clarity; knowing beyond the personal, the ego, the little 'I'. .

As I look back on these lives, I acknowledge that I have long sought the gift of love. For love is a gift. Little did I know that this gift which I have searched for high and low, life after life, love after painful love would prove so elusive, so intangible. Perhaps this gift of love would be revealed in the story of the 7th chakra for this is, after all, the master switch, the transformer...

It struck me as a very unusual way of addressing my love life, or lack of, in this current incarnation, but as I began to remember these lifetimes, I realized that I had experienced so much loss around love. Even back then...no wonder I was scared, petrified, in fact, to try again. It was as though I had everything to lose.

Did I make a decision on a soul level that romantic love is too messy, relationships too painful, finding the love of my life too heart-breaking to go through yet again?

Is that why I remain unmarried in this lifetime? My own soul put on the brakes and said "No way." It's possible.

Even though I had uncovered many unanswered questions about relationships and my quest for love in these first six chakras (or lifetimes), I still had issues...unresolved puzzles that sat in my heart. There was clearly more to learn.

Who knows the twists and turns of fate? I only know that I had been through so much in these other lives. Each life had its own rhythm and purpose; some might say they were tragic and I was overdue for some happiness. I won't argue with that.

Even though I could look down that long road of remembering and thus claim the title of mystic, more questions remained.

My current life, for example, seemed to exemplify the qualities of the 7th chakra, the crown; linked to the heavens, feet barely on the ground. Well, that *sums me up! I wondered if this life now held the answers.*

I would have to dig deep and present the stories in a way that would be palatable...perhaps I would write about this life under a pen name...Arianna Black, my alter ego...yes, that is the way forward.

Watch for the continuing evolution of the chakras as these lives merge in "Convergence"...the tale of the 7th chakra.